loud world, quiet thoughts

by david jones

Copyright © David Jones, 2019.

All rights reserved.

This book is sold subject to the condition that it shall not, by way of trade or otherwise be lent, resold, hired out, or otherwise circulated without the publisher's prior consent in any form of binding or cover other than that in which it is published and without a similar condition, including this condition, being imposed upon the subsequent purchaser.

loud world, quiet thoughts

contents

part i............................ loud world
part ii.......................quiet thoughts

loud world

loud world, quiet thoughts

let's meet again, for the first time.

in the end you learn when to let go, and when to hold on.

loud world, quiet thoughts

say it before it's too late.

deep down, you always knew.

- a five word short story

loud world, quiet thoughts

find the one you can talk to, when you can't talk to anyone else.

if it hurts, then it's teaching.

i didn't ask, because i was scared of the answer.

i didn't speak to you, because i hoped you'd speak to me.

loud world, quiet thoughts

find someone who makes you smile, even when you don't want to.

i never knew how easy it was, to be happy and sad at the same time.

the more you care, the more it hurts.

- an eight word short story

sometimes the heart knows before the mind realises.

loud world, quiet thoughts

a break on the inside, doesn't always show on the outside.

one day you will find the right person, the right time: the right love.

loud world, quiet thoughts

it wasn't a surprise, but it still hurt.

who you want, and who you need, are sometimes two different people.

loud world, quiet thoughts

let go of the ones who let go of you.

sometimes goodbye really is forever.

- a five word short story.

forget the person, but not the lesson.

maybe one day we'll travel the world together.

- an eight word short story.

loud world, quiet thoughts

and i'll miss you, without saying a word.

and in the end, some people just aren't meant to be.

but fate knew something that we didn't.

- a seven word short story.

fight for the ones who would fight for you.

loud world, quiet thoughts

if they walk away, don't run after them.

the right person, but the wrong time.

- a seven word short story.

loud world, quiet thoughts

win the silent battles.

if only not seeing you, meant not missing you.

loud world, quiet thoughts

don't mistake the end of the chapter for the end of the story.

everything goes deeper than you think.

loud world, quiet thoughts

remember to live while you're busy surviving.

if it isn't a happy ending yet, keep writing.

loud world, quiet thoughts

we found each other at the wrong time.

- an eight word short story.

better to feel too much, than nothing at all.

a beginning

eyes meet, and then look away.

you are gone, but what i felt is still here.

loud world, quiet thoughts

maybe.

- the story of you and i.

the thing that broke you, won't heal you.

loud world, quiet thoughts

a story of modern love

two people, neither wanting to text first.

the more it hurt, the more it taught.

loud world, quiet thoughts

everything seems sweeter, after it's gone.

the struggle between holding on, and letting go.

loud world, quiet thoughts

if only we could meet again, for the first time.

they never tell you how long it takes to forget.

loud world, quiet thoughts

i don't know what love is, but sometimes it means having to forget.

some leave marks, others leave scars.

from lovers, to strangers.

- a four word short story.

like the sun to the moon, i'll miss you at dawn.

we said goodbye, but i never knew why.

- an eight word short story.

if you can't forget it, make peace with it.

loud world, quiet thoughts

i hope the story ends with "you and i."

my heart continues writing, long after the story has ended.

loud world, quiet thoughts

if you have to chase them, they've already gone.

try to please everyone and you'll end up disappointed.

loud world, quiet thoughts

let go. make room. it's how life works.

try not to take your pain out on the world.

loud world, quiet thoughts

the things you got through, made you.

was it all for nothing?

- a five word short story.

loud world, quiet thoughts

and after all, we were never meant for each other.

in the end, time got the better of us.

- a nine word short story.

loud world, quiet thoughts

don't fall in love with an impossibility.

sometimes home can be another person.

loud world, quiet thoughts

and in a dream, my hand finds yours.

i let go of you so that i could hold onto me.

loud world, quiet thoughts

funny, how the heart is heavier after the breaks.

how can we go from loving each other, to hurting each other?

just another day without you.

- a six word short story.

once you were gone, i realised that you were never really here.

loud world, quiet thoughts

people care more about broken bones, than broken minds.

i fell in love with a distant star.

i wish it had been us.

- a six word short story.

i realised i could live without you, after all.

loud world, quiet thoughts

life is a dance of love and loss.

how can i believe, that there will be another you?

loud world, quiet thoughts

that simple forever. i swear it killed me.

every day, you survive.

- a four word short story.

loud world, quiet thoughts

all i wish, is that we'd found each other sooner.

sometimes the broken pieces make a stronger whole.

and now you are someone else's dream.

- a seven word short story.

heal your heart. everything else will follow.

loud world, quiet thoughts

dreams never tell lies.

- a four word short story.

i dreamed of you long before we even met.

let's have forever, for a moment.

- a six word short story.

you ask yourself again and again:

"what did i do to deserve this?"

but never suspect that the answer is:

"nothing."

why? her.

- a two word short story.

i never knew, that i'd been waiting for you.

loud world, quiet thoughts

the love you deserve is out there, somewhere.

i lost you before you were gone.

loud world, quiet thoughts

you can't go back, so go forward.

i knew i'd miss you.

- a five word short story.

loud world, quiet thoughts

let love find you.

you'll always be the one i look for in a crowd.

loud world, quiet thoughts

what broke your heart so much that you swore you would never let anyone in ever again?

i dreamed of you before i even knew who you were.

loud world, quiet thoughts

type out a message to you. delete. repeat.

- an eight word short story.

sometimes the deadliest poisons taste the sweetest.

loud world, quiet thoughts

if you know you're going to have to start forgetting, better to begin sooner rather than later.

there are two types of forever. the happy, and the sad ending.

loud world, quiet thoughts

don't be afraid to grow.

i seemed to be lost but i was busy finding myself.

i wanted to say, i miss you.

- a seven word short story.

life is full of sad things. all we can do is try and find some meaning amongst the sadness.

loud world, quiet thoughts

but all the songs i used to love, remind me of you.

seek out the love you deserve.

loud world, quiet thoughts

keep wandering.

quiet thoughts

the rule
of life is:

let it
happen.

people
come and
go.

life goes
on.

find someone
who deserves you,
not just
wants
you.

i loved
you, lost
you.

the end.

loud world, quiet thoughts

oh to
start again
in a new place
with a new
heart.

you will
always be,
the last
dream that
i dream.

loud world, quiet thoughts

a simple
truth:

you are
already
enough.

how easy
it is,
to lose
yourself in
someone
else.

loud world, quiet thoughts

the things
we love
the most,
hurt us
the most.

a truth?

we'll never
have today
again.

you dream
of where your
heart wants
to be.

and
in the end
all i learned
was how
to be strong
alone.

loud world, quiet thoughts

we need
both the sun
and the rain
to grow.

i loved you
even when
it hurt.

loud world, quiet thoughts

let an end
become
a beginning.

remember:
you will never
have these days
again.

loud world, quiet thoughts

and sometimes
we wait,
long after
they have

gone.

and of course
something
must end
for something
to begin.

loud world, quiet thoughts

forget
the ones who
forget
you.

fell asleep
in love with
you.

woke up
in love with
you.

sometimes
things end
long before
they begin.

i told the
stars about
you.

loud world, quiet thoughts

spring exists
to remind us that
everything can
begin
again.

i am so
lost because
you felt like
home.

loud world, quiet thoughts

i fell
for you
and i am
still
falling.

your arms
are the
only place
i want
to be.

love yourself
before you
love another.

do i
miss you,
or do i
miss who
i was

with you?

the problem is,
i would still
choose you,
over anyone
and

anything.

learn to
love without
hope.

"end" is
just another
word for
"beginning."

there was
a life before,
and after,

you.

loud world, quiet thoughts

we wish
for forever,
when all
we have
is now.

**we were
so close to
forever.**

whatever you
didn't do:
do it now.

whatever you
didn't say
say it now.

ends are
often written
before
beginnings.

loud world, quiet thoughts

without
the darkness,
we would
never see
the stars.

unspoken
words are
often the
loudest.

loud world, quiet thoughts

were the
bad times worth
the good?

the pain
of the end,
brings the
peace of the
beginning.

loud world, quiet thoughts

tears
tell untold
stories.

sometimes
we have to be
broken
to be repaired.

loud world, quiet thoughts

under the moon
anything
seems possible.

even
you.

a broken heart
is stronger
after the
break.

a word
can change
a day.

a book
can change
a life.

broken?
no, just
rearranging.

and how
could i have
guessed?

there was life
after you.

so much
life.

my dreams
still belong
to you.

loud world, quiet thoughts

you still live in
the silences
between
my thoughts.

surviving
is easy.
living
is harder.

loud world, quiet thoughts

i listen to
the silence
and hear
your
voice.

i don't regret
losing you,
but

losing
me.

loud world, quiet thoughts

i look into
your eyes and
hope to
see

the rest of
my life.

don't wait
for time
to heal.

start now.

More About the Author.

David Jones is an internationally best selling author living in Liverpool, UK. He has published both poetry and prose, and his books are known to explore the deeper feelings of life, emotions we have all felt and experiences we have all been through. People across the world identify strongly with his words and often find comfort within the pages of his books.

His poetry books have enjoyed tremendous success, often ranking as best sellers across the world. He has enjoyed a great deal of popularity on social media, and his writing has variously been posted by celebrities including Cara Delevingne, Khloe Kardashian, Britney Spears and Camilla Cabelo. He has also worked on academic projects and is currently completing a thesis in Early Modern travel writing at the University of Liverpool. His writing has been greeted with critical acclaim, and he is currently working on a full, feature length novel exploring themes of love, eternity, the nature of the universe and history.

As well as writing and publishing books, David also writes scripts for theatre, acts and recently returned from a successful run as part of a comedy sketch troupe at the Edinburgh Festival. He also writes and directs short films, as well as uploading to his Youtube channel. David can be found on Facebook, Twitter @djthedavid, Instagram @storydj and on Youtube at youtube.com/storydj.

Blog, gifts and competitions: www.patreon.com/storydj

More Books.

Love and Space Dust.

Love & Space Dust is a poetry anthology exploring love and eternity. Timeless poetry of feeling and emotion, Love & Space Dust carries readers on a journey through love, life and relationships, and then far beyond, into the stars and the far flung galaxies, where all that remains of the feelings we once felt and the lives we once lived is love and space dust.

"After spending over ten years in a literature club and hearing/reading more poems than I could count, I thought I had seen it all. I have never been so wrong. Love and Space Dust contains so many beautifully written poems that brought tears to my eyes that I didn't put my Kindle down until I had read every single one of them at least twice." Amazon.de Customer Review.

"Lovely book." Amazon.com Customer Review.

"I really enjoy all of the poems. They make you feel like never before. By far some of my favorite poems." Amazon.com Customer Review.

"LOVED LOVED LOVED THIS!!" Goodreads Review.

"These poems are so full of Pain and Darkness, but so full of Hope and Light." Amazon.de Customer Review.

"This book is absolutely amazing and i hope there will be more to come!" Amazon.com Customer Review.

"Love this book so much!" Goodreads Review.

"Made me smile and moved me to tears." Amazon.co.uk Customer Review.

Could You Ever Live Without?

Poems of feeling and experience, the anthology encompasses all of life and beyond: death, the universe, hopes, dreams, love, loss - all of existence contained in one work. Poetry that captures both moments and lifetimes, memories and hopes, reality and dreams. Poems to identify with, poems of life.

"Take it from a non-poetry reader: this book is a gem, destined to become timeless." Amazon Customer Review.

"Loved the poems, a very great read. Once I started reading it was hard to stop." Amazon Customer Review.

"This book is beautiful. It's one of my most cherished possessions." Amazon Customer Review.

"Not all poetry is worth reading. This is." Amazon Customer Review.

"A great reflection of the deeper thoughts from this generation." Amazon Customer Review.

"Beautiful collection of poetry, I'm not an avid poetry reader but this book is absolutely stunning." Amazon.co.uk Customer Review.

"Everytime I read this book I find new meanings." Goodreads Review.

Love As The Stars Went Out.

A collection of poetry from the end of the world. Poems of love, feeling and emotion, the collection encompasses all of life, and even beyond. Simple and elegant, the book contains all the poetry of existence.

"This book is amazing I would really recommend getting the other two as well they are some of my favourite books of all time." Amazon.co.uk Customer Review.

"I love every bit of this book. So simple yet deep meaningful words. I would recommend it to all and everyone...." Amazon.com Customer Review.

"Five stars. Awesome book." Amazon.com Customer Review.

"Such a beautiful piece." Amazon.com Customer Review.

Death's Door.

"She was like the dawn, insubstantial and somehow transient, as though she would fade from reality at any moment."

Every day the villagers watch as Death, a spectral suit of black armour mounted upon a horse, rides through the valley beneath their mountain top home. After a lifetime living on the edge of Death's domain, his close proximity is neither terrible or threatening, rather he has become a simple fact of life and a familiar neighbour. Nothing seems to change until one night a young boy, alone in the meadows beneath a summer moon, watches a mysterious figure in white approaching the village through the tall grass.

"A spectacular novella, a quick read but engaging and thoughtful. The story carries you as swift as death's horse does." Amazon.com Customer Review.

"Buy this book! Great teen-based book. Even better for post teen (aka 55 year old father) reader." Amazon.com Customer Review.

"This book quickly became my forever favourite. You will not regret buying it. Although it's about death himself, it has so much to teach about life." Amazon.com Customer Review.

Moonlight & You.

"You were never my dream to dream."

Moonlight And You is not only about dreams, but what remains of those dreams after the dawn, and what is left of our wildest hopes, our most vivid fantasies and our fairytale loves. The book explores themes of love, relationships, heartbreak and loss but also hope, and the search for happiness. Its setting is ethereal night's beneath the moon, when time stands still and anything in the world seems possible.

Moonlight And You blurs the boundaries between love, dreams and reality. It delves into our dreams, and how we might hold onto them after the embers of the dawn.

"I love this book! Beautiful read. Five stars." Amazon Customer Review.

Highway Heart.

Highway Heart is a collection of over one hundred poems on relationships, life and the universe. The theme is journeys - the travel we undertake in life, the type of internal travel which traces roads inside our hearts.

Half an exploration of the difficulties of finding the right path in life, and half a bitter sweet celebration of the myriad of strange, exciting, heartbreaking and unexpected roads we discover for ourselves, Highway Heart is above all else the poetic tale of a journey.

"This is one of the greatest works I've ever read. This is truly, truly, a masterpiece. I hope it gets more recognition in the future. Please, please read it, it will touch the deepest parts of your heart." Amazon.com Review.

loud world, quiet thoughts

Made in the USA
Monee, IL
12 September 2023

42619174R00100